A Glass of Fresh Air

Collected by Moira Andrew
Illustrated by Meena Arnold

CollinsEducational
An Imprint of HarperCollinsPublishers

CONTENTS

Standing Here On Earth

Prayer to the Sun	5
Haiku	6
Full	6
Drought	7
Flamenco	8
Dead Rainbows	9
Brighter Later	10

With A Lick Of Its Tongue

What is Water?	13
Exploring the Rock Pool	14
The Coast	15
High Tide, Ebb Tide	15
Weep with the Whale	16
Newlyn Bay	17

A Space To Breathe

Croc's Lament	19
Tall Story	20
A Giraffe's Tears	21
At the End of a School Day	22
Sealsong	23
Night Prowler	24
Foxy	25

Amazed At Cowslips

Strongholds	27
City Bees	28
Spring into Action	29
Nature Study	30
The Butterfly	31
River	32
Dragonflies	33

From Bough To Bough

Top Floor	35
The Day the Bulldozers Came	36
Fireweed in the Park	37
Predator	38
A Glass of Fresh Air	39

The World Is Singing

The World is Singing	41
The Backs of Houses	42
Magic	43
Quiet	44
Night Fishing	45
First Snow of Winter	46
A Poem to be Spoken Silently	47
Daisies	48

Prayer to the Sun

Give me my blue sky for ever,
ancient man with the lit face.
Give me my white cloud over and over,
old soul with the flaming head.
Give me your golden shelter for ever,
great knife of gold in whose gleam
we stand here on earth.

Indian poem from the Argentinean pampas,
translated from a Spanish version

Roger Garfitt

Haiku

No-one's spoilt it yet.
Dare I be the first to use
This bright morning?

Pam Gidney

Full

The day's
as full of possibilities
as of light.

Sun high already
cutting the mist apart
under shadowed trees.

Rupert M Loydell

Drought

Sun hot
Hasn't rained
No water
Walked miles
But water's mud
River's dry
Can't bathe
Can't drink
Brown grass
No grass
Skeletons stare
From cracked earth.

And then one morning
Without a warning
The sound of rain
A stranger tapping
Pitter pattering
Onto our rooftops
Into our pails
Giving birth to streams
Filling our rivers
Feeding the cattle
The sound of rain.

We're all smiling
Children running naked
Mouths open towards the Gods
We're all laughing
Me forgetting to hide
The gap between my teeth.

Accabre Huntley

Flamenco

Days dance into summer
wearing new green shoes
and yellow skirts, toes
tapping to tambourines
shaken in the treetops.

Moira Andrew

Dead Rainbows

Outside in the playground,
Jane stood staring sad-eyed down
At something sorrowful she'd found.

I was curious and so
I joined her; she pointed with a frown:

"Look," eyes on a glistening oil puddle,
"A rainbow lying dead on the ground."

David R Morgan

Brighter Later

      and some of all
that rain
      that was falling
      that November day
      fell and daubed black
      the line of bare trees
      and some of all
that rain
      shivered
      onto the steep
      slate roofs
      of the row's
      few houses
      and some of all
that rain
      skidded into
      the cast iron gutters
      and tumbled
      the length
      of the cast-iron downpipes
      and some of all
that rain
      slopped into the several
      buckets and butts
      placed there
      for the purpose

and some of all
that rain
    filled
    to overflowing
    one dark blue bucket
    underneath which
    in a stone-dry ring
    as some of all
that rain
    flopped over its rim
    crept –
    slow as the sun
    was crossing the sky –
    one ladybird's
    small flame

David Horner

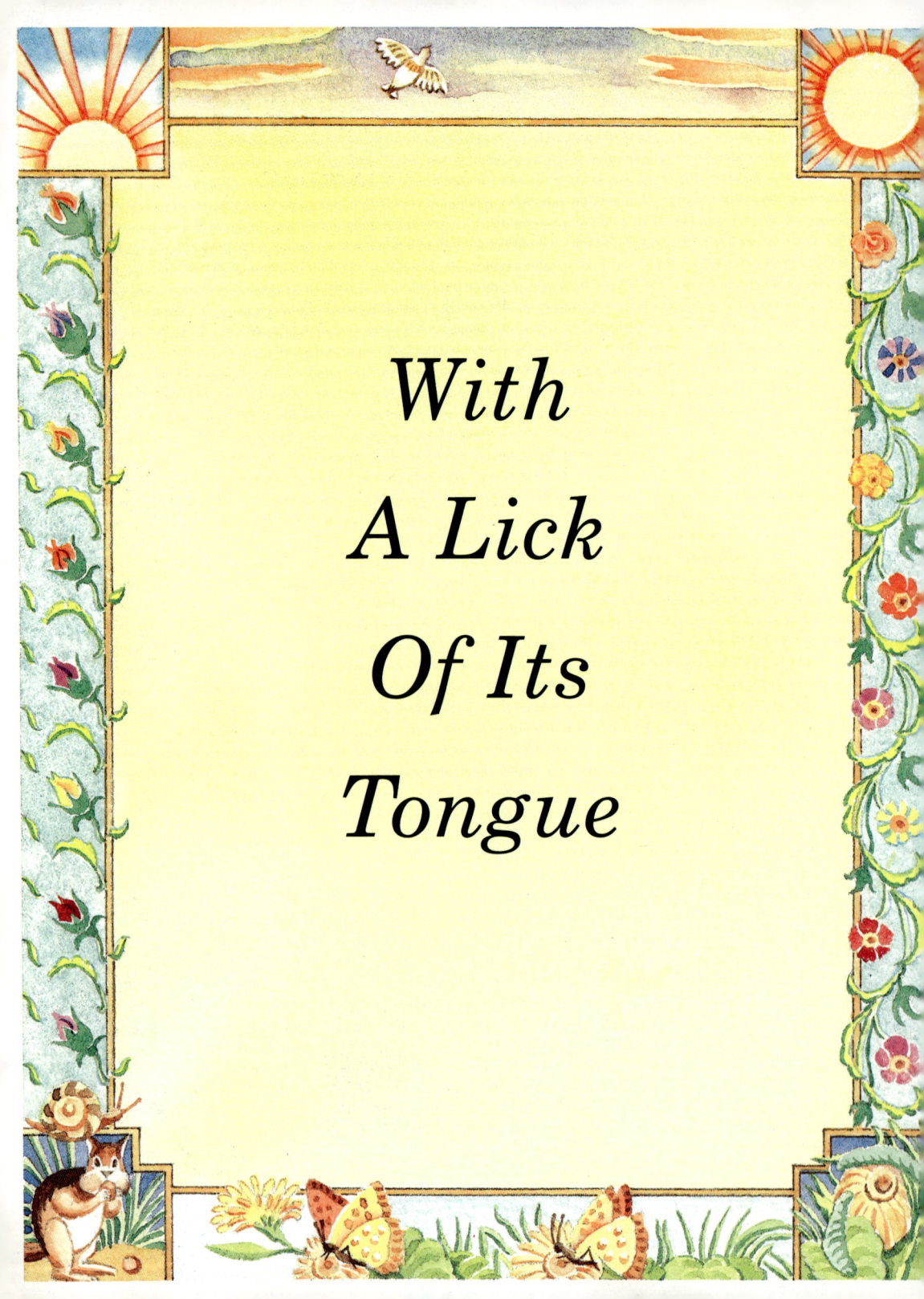

With A Lick Of Its Tongue

What is Water?

A magician
Transforming deserts
With a lick of its tongue.

A conjuror
Coating ponds with ice
Or brushing your cheek with mist.

A wild animal
Plunging over cliffs,
Breaking bridges and flooding valleys.

A healer
Quenching thirst,
Rekindling the seeds' flame.

A slippery customer
Slithering through your fingers,
Always on the run.

John Foster

Exploring the Rock Pool

We explore the rock pool,
A small world of its own:
The scuttling crab, quick shrimps,
Sea-polished stone
With hints of colours
Enhanced by the light-
Refracting water
Making all so bright.
The strands of seaweed
Verdant, sleek as silk,
The tiny limpets'
Shells as white as milk.
A sea in miniature
Which lasts just for a day,
When the tide renews it
Washing the old away.

John Cotton

The Coast

Beaches grumble as summer storms in
with wellingtons, sandals, picnic baskets,
blankets, canned drinks and dogs.

Beaches grumble as lolly sticks,
tin cans, beer bottles, disposable nappies
are left with sand castles for the incoming tide.

Beaches relax as night falls,
a jade curtain of sea creeps forward,
soaking out coffee and icecream stains.

Beaches relax as sun bleeds into ocean,
its pattern a gentle cooling,
a quiet sky backdrop.

Beaches breathe in dark night air,
rest in pebbled certainty
of visitors again next day.

Sue Moules

High Tide, Ebb Tide

                Hooligan sea
        Heaving flotsam
At the beach.

Swaggering retreat.
        Rattling applause
                Of pebbles.

John Coldwell

Weep with the Whale

The great grey bodies
swing and twist with
slow grace, like Olympic
gymnasts in an action
      replay.

Their songs are the
mournful mouth-music
of the deep, pitched
thin and high with
      sadness.

Joined in an underwater
ceilidh, their keening
echoes on the waves
like a lament for the
      future.

Moira Andrew

Newlyn Bay

We look down on
fishing boats
    t
     e
      t
       h
        e
         r
          e
           d
to the harbour wall,
their riding lights
    flickering
  like fireflies
in the summer dark.

They dip and curtsey
like a corps de ballet
      n c i
    a   n
  d   g
  to the tune
  of the waves.

Moira Andrew

A Space To Breathe

Croc's Lament

A crocodile
Will rarely smile,
She knows your plans are drastic.
She will save her skin
With a mirthless grin
And suggest you use some plastic.

Trevor Millum

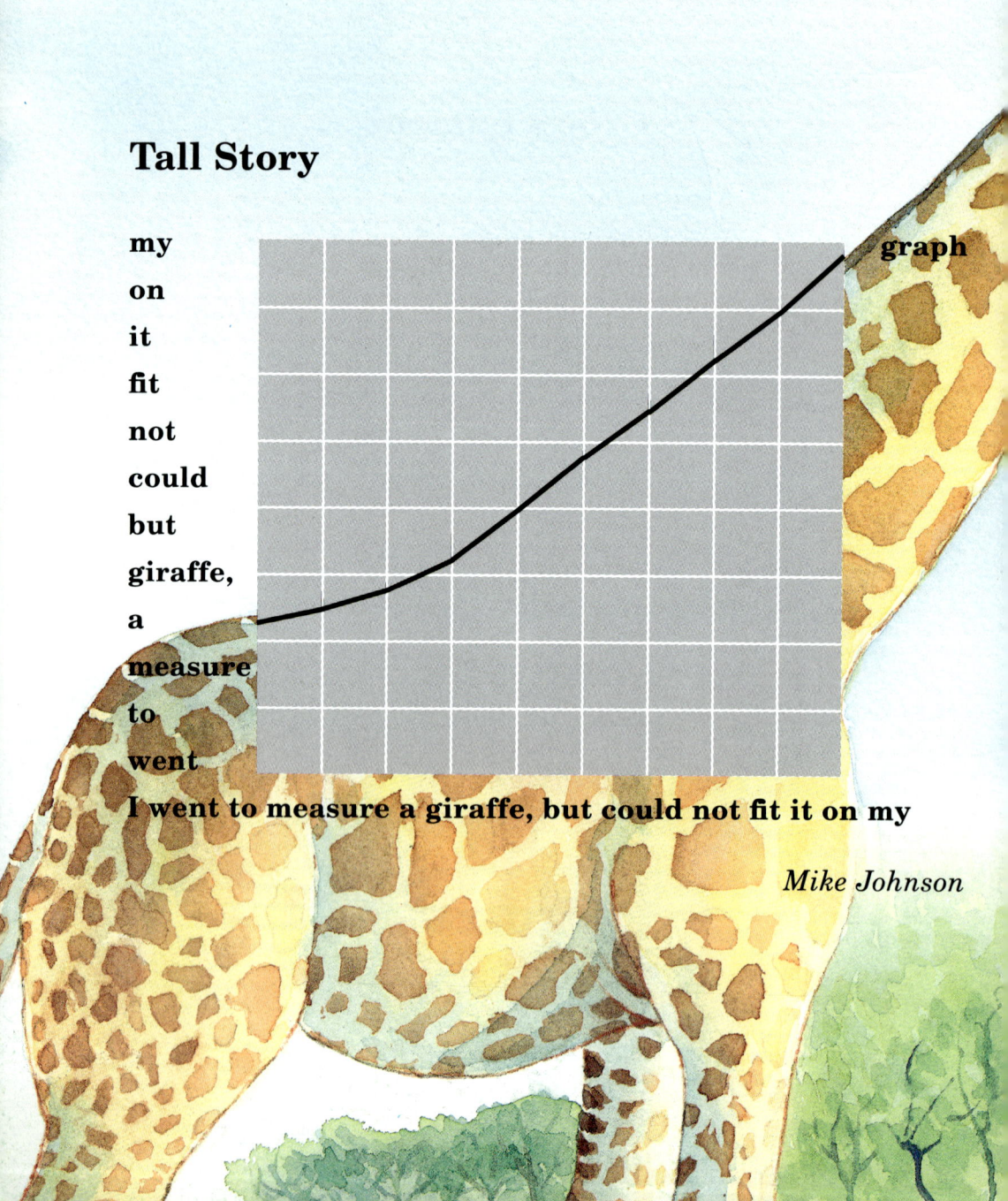

Tall Story

my on it fit not could but giraffe, a measure to went graph

I went to measure a giraffe, but could not fit it on my

Mike Johnson

A Giraffe's Tears

A giraffe's tears are different,
they're the biggest in the world,
bigger than a crocodile's

and so much further to fall.

Katherine Gallagher

At the End of a School Day

It is the end of a school day
    and down the long drive
come bag-swinging, shouting children.
    Deafened, the sky winces.
        The sun gapes in surprise.

Suddenly the runners skid to a stop,
    stand still and stare
at a small hedgehog
    curled up on the tarmac
        like an old, frayed cricket ball.

A girl dumps her bag, tiptoes forward
    and gingerly, so gingerly,
carries the creature
    to the safety of a shady hedge.
        Then steps back, watching.

Girl, children, sky and sun
    hold their breath.
There is a silence,
    a moment to remember
        on this warm afternoon in June.

Wes Magee

Sealsong

Around me, seas
stretch endlessly;
above me, sky.
A space to breathe,
a place to swim;
to pace the days
by moon or sun.
A place that time
had kept from man;

no place to die.

Judith Nicholls

Night Prowler

Skulking round the dustbins,
Flame-red in dead of night,
Sharp-pricked ears, dark plume of a tail –
Urban fox on the backstreet trail.

Jennifer Curry

Foxy

Surefooted and silent,
something's slinking
through oil-thick blackness.

Fox is out!

Hedges shiver and, fields away,
a white goose stiffens,
hens bristle, fidget their feathers.

Fox knows where he's going!

See! there! Quick as a blink,
caught in our headlamps,
the ghost-gems of his eyes!

Matt Simpson

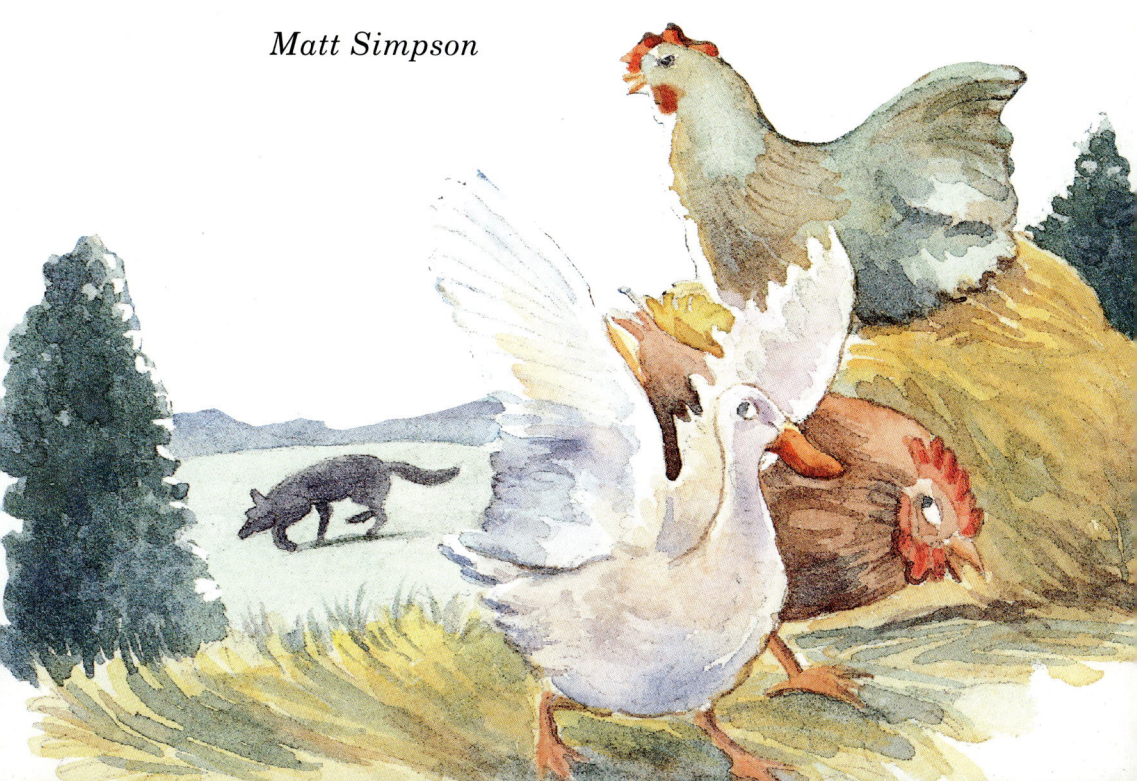

Amazed At Cowslips

Strongholds

We are on Hod Hill,
amazed at cowslips
we must not pick.

Our fingers itch.

Butterflies
lead our eyes a dance.
Orange tips, blues
and marbled whites.
We count them
on our fingers
and this year
need two hands.

Mary Maher

City Bees

In a drab back yard
At the back of the shop
Among boxes and bins
A world away
From flowering fields
And hedgerows in blossom
Mr Patel keeps bees.

City bees.
They browse on buddleia and
Ragged weeds
Rosebay willowherb
And dust-heavy trees
But their busy wings
Bring sweetness
To the city.

Jennifer Curry

Spring into Action

Spring starts off an AWFUL MESS.
Sure as clockwork, we can guess
The type of weather we shall see
Is MUD and SLUSH and PLANT DEBRIS
Left by Winter in its wake;
So, COME ON DAFFS, give Spring a BREAK!
GROW UP, you bulbs, and show your face
To rescue Spring from such disgrace.
O.K. YOU TREES? Enough of rootin' –
Just give the order:
      "BUDS – START SHOOTIN'!"

Trevor Harvey

Nature Study

This butterfly
we couldn't identify
    pitched
its bright tent
on a roadside flower.

For a full minute
outstretched wings
    bloodied
the morning air
in studied symmetry.

Our eyes ached
with raw colour,
    remembered
pattern and shape
against eventual flight.

It drifted away
and precise geometry
    lingered
like an after-image
in the yellow heat.

    Moira Andrew

The Butterfly

I always think the butterfly
Looks best against the clear blue sky;
I do not think he looks so good
Pinned down within a box of wood.

Anon

River

Dragonflies snatch at light,
spin it into colour.
Hover above water,
reflecting the spectrum.
Rippled glow,
stonesplash gurgle,
spilling downstream,
swallowing light
as wings carry them off —
blue-green specks in the wind.

Rupert M Loydell

Dragonflies

They used to fly
over all the ponds
in summer, Granny says –

like sparkling sapphire helicopters,
purple aeroplanes,
with eyes of bright topaz,
wings flashing emerald light,
brightening the countryside
in their jewelled flight.

Sun-glow brilliance winging
over every pond,
someday I hope to see one
– smallest last dragon.

Joan Poulson

From Bough To Bough

Top Floor

Once, they say, you could have swung
From bough to bough from one end of England
To the other – crossing the rivers
Where boughs shook hands across a narrower part.

Now only the ground floor's left,
But we needed the fires, the houses,
Beds, chairs, tables,
Pit-props, fences, farm carts,
Schools, shops and ships
That were made from those trees,
Didn't we?

Stanley Cook

The Day the Bulldozers Came

The day the bulldozers came
Rooks were building
Crazy egg baskets in the oaks;
Green flies sizzled by the pond
And a cold-eyed toad
Waited for them.

The day the bulldozers came
Squirrels were scattering
Up tree trunks,
And leapt from branches
That were hardly there.

The fox
Stirred in his sleep
As the ground trembled
      "Ha Ha!" he thought,
        "I'm quite safe,
Deep down in the Earth,
No-one can get me here."

Then the bulldozers came.

        David Orme

Fireweed in the Park

The park keeper hates us,
For we sneak out when he's not looking
And tell scarlet stories so shocking
That all the dusty old women
Start sneezing at once;
So they trap the park keeper
In his hut,
Bang on the door with their sticks,
Shout through his letterbox,
And threaten to do him a mischief.
He rushes out in a rage
And chops and slashes and burns
And thinks he's done the trick.

What a laugh!
For we've all grown feathers,
Turned into a flock of white doves
And flown high over the fence.

Now we must look for earth,
Earth as dark as a magician's hat.

David Orme

Predator

The wind is a wolf,
grey sleet dripping
from its fangs. It
tears wild-eyed at
trees, spitting out
branches like gnawed
chicken bones.

Moira Andrew

A Glass of Fresh Air

Early last Sunday morning,
Dad announced we needed a glass of fresh air
and a mouthful of greenness;
so off we slipped to the nearby park
where we crept in as soundless as snails.
Around us the day breathed air
that was as sharp as vinegar,
reminding us that winter was well on its way.

Inside, as the wind rudely pushed past us,
we watched the trees stretch and wake
while the grass stood up and shivered.
Soon, I was pointing towards a spider
that was strung on a necklace web
from which delicately hung –
the morning's golden jewel – the sun.

Dad smiled
while his eyes led me to where
a squirrel scampered from a bush
then turned to grey stone,
until with a flick of its tail,
it joined a passing breeze and was gone.

Later as we passed the children's playground,
I stopped and stared at the solitary red slide,
and for a moment remembered the summer days
when I had flown its long slippery tongue;
but a tug of wind pulled me on past
until I let the warmth in Dad's hand
lead me on towards home.

Ian Souter

The World Is Singing

The World is Singing

the world is singing
let us sing

the world is spinning
let us spin

the world turns, dreaming
let us turn dreams

let us not cry
for a dying world

for if we
sing and spin our dreams

this is not the end
this is only
the beginning

Dave Ward

The Backs of Houses

From a train you see
the backs of houses
junkyards of factories
edges of allotments
where Brussels sprouts
grow tall and yellow.

Cars die in secret places
at the scrag ends of gardens
dried up growths
go to seed behind sheds
where rubbish blows
uncollected.

Rita Ray

Magic

A web
captures the storm:
glass beads, safe in fine net,
gather sunlight as they sway in
high winds.

Judith Nicholls

Quiet

Once there was quiet in the valley,
We could hear the slow thoughts of mountains,
The breathing of small hills,
And at evening the dark forest trees listening to the silence.
Then came the traffic
And it was never the same.
The Earth stopped hearing
And the still, small voices were drowned,
Though sometimes in the early pre-dawn hours
The quiet will pay its secret visits
From where it waits.

John Cotton

Night Fishing

If stars were minnows,
they would flash across
the river of night, hiding
in its dark waters from
Fisherman-in-the-moon.

Moira Andrew

First Snow of Winter

We wake to a world bewitched,
a black and white negative
of itself. Hunchback gardens
crouch beneath the gun-grey sky
like a flock of gulls
huddled shoulder to shoulder
on some salty shoreline.

Feathered trees thrust out
bare branches, wide as wings,
across the bleak horizon.
Blackbirds balance on the
snow-sheathed fence, their
beaks ripping bright holes
in the colourless morning.

Moira Andrew

A Poem to be Spoken Silently

It was so silent that I heard
my thoughts rustle
like leaves in a paper bag...

It was so peaceful that I heard
the trees ease off
their coats of bark...

It was so still that I felt
a raindrop's grin
as it tickled the window pane...

It was so silent that I heard
a page in this book
whisper to its neighbour,
"Look, he's peering at us again..."

It was so quiet that I sensed
a smile crack the face
of a stranger...

It was so hushed that I heard
the morning earth roll over
in its sleep and doze
for five minutes more...

Pie Corbett

Daisies

Just when I think
that the world has gone crazy,
I open my eyes
and the lawn's full of daisies!

Theresa Heine